Adobe

# ADOBE

ODYSSEYS

MARI BOLTE

CREATIVE EDUCATION · CREATIVE PAPERBACKS

Published by Creative Education and Creative Paperbacks
P.O. Box 227, Mankato, Minnesota 56002
Creative Education and Creative Paperbacks are imprints of
The Creative Company
www.thecreativecompany.us

Design by Blue Design
Art direction by Tom Morgan

Images by Adobe InDesign, 70–71; Adobe Photoshop, cover; Adobe Sigma, 69; AI generated/Dan Saelinger, 64, Pablo Xavier, 75; Dreamstime/Hugo Kurk, 53, Michaelvi, 50, Wellesenterprises, 2; flickr/Web Summit, 6, 46, 58, 60; Getty Images/Ann E. Yow-Dyson, 9, Bernard Bisson, 19, Chip Somodevilla, 41, Ed Maker, 11, Ethan Miller, 26, Roger Ressmeyer/Corbis, 16; Microsoft Copilot, 66; Unsplash/Kelsey Todd, 54, Museums Victoria, 24–25; Wikimedia Commons/Adobe Systems, 20, Claude Garamond / Printers working for the Plantin-Moretus Museum, 28, en:User:GearedBull, 4–5, Felix Winkelnkemper, 32, Koreller, 31, Mathew Benjamin Brady, 63, Web Summit, 34



Library of Congress Cataloging-in-Publication Data

Names: Bolte, Mari author
Title: Adobe / by: Mari Bolte.
Description: Mankato, Minnesota : Creative Education and Creative Paperbacks, [2026] | Series: Odysseys in business | Includes bibliographical references and index. | Audience: Ages 12-15 | Audience: Grades 7-9 | Summary: "Discover Adobe's journey of revolutionizing design with tools like Photoshop and Illustrator. Perfect for high school creatives eager to learn how Adobe inspires innovation worldwide. This title includes sidebars, a glossary, selected bibliography, websites, and an index"-- Provided by publisher.
Identifiers: LCCN 2025021155 (print) | LCCN 2025021156 (ebook) | ISBN 9798895811320 library binding | ISBN 9798896800859 paperback | ISBN 9798895812587 ebook
Subjects: LCSH: Adobe Inc—History—Juvenile literature | Adobe Systems—History—Juvenile literature | Desktop publishing industry—Juvenile literature
Classification: LCC Z244.64 .B65 2025 (print) | LCC Z244.64 (ebook) | DDC 005.52--dc23/eng/20250806
LC record available at https://lccn.loc.gov/2025021155
LC ebook record available at https://lccn.loc.gov/2025021156

Printed in the United States

*r*

a

ANON

hijklm

uvwxyz

456789

## CONTENTS

**Introduction** . . . . . . . . . . . . . . . . . . . . . . . **9**

**Changing the World** . . . . . . . . . . . . . . . . . . **13**

Out of Toner . . . . . . . . . . . . . . . . . . . . . . . . . 23

The Font Wars . . . . . . . . . . . . . . . . . . . . . . . . 28

**Save As** . . . . . . . . . . . . . . . . . . . . . . . . . . **35**

For Ransom . . . . . . . . . . . . . . . . . . . . . . . . . 39

Fortune 500 . . . . . . . . . . . . . . . . . . . . . . . . . 45

**Innovations** . . . . . . . . . . . . . . . . . . . . . . . . **48**

Data Farms . . . . . . . . . . . . . . . . . . . . . . . . . 53

Buying Power . . . . . . . . . . . . . . . . . . . . . . . . 58

**Toward the Future** . . . . . . . . . . . . . . . . . . . **61**

I Photoshopped It . . . . . . . . . . . . . . . . . . . . . 63

Photoshop Ethics . . . . . . . . . . . . . . . . . . . . . . 75

**Selected Bibliography** . . . . . . . . . . . . . . . . . **76**

**Glossary** . . . . . . . . . . . . . . . . . . . . . . . . . . **77**

**Websites** . . . . . . . . . . . . . . . . . . . . . . . . . . **79**

**Index** . . . . . . . . . . . . . . . . . . . . . . . . . . . . **80**

# Introduction

In March 1999, more than a thousand participants gathered at the Hyatt Regency Hotel in San Francisco, California, for the Seybold Conference, an event for publishing professionals. They were there to attend seminars, see product demonstrations, and meet industry **analysts**. They were waiting for an epic showdown between two of the biggest **desktop publishing** companies in the industry: Quark and Adobe.

**OPPOSITE:** John Warnock, one of the founders of Adobe.

At the 1998 Seybold Conference, Apple CEO Steve Jobs brought representatives from both companies onstage to show how their software worked with the latest Mac computer. Tim Gill, Quark's chief technology officer, stepped up, raved about Apple's newest operating system, and quickly handed the microphone back. Then, it was Adobe's turn. Ben Vanderberg, the InDesign product manager, gave the crowd a taste of the company's newest technology, a program codenamed K2.

The year before, Quark had offered to buy Adobe. Adobe was at least twice its size. Adobe laughed off the offer and came to Seybold with a response—the launch of K2, now officially titled InDesign. Publishing professionals called the program the "Quark Killer."

"Adobe InDesign is here," MacWeek wrote. "Graphic design software is about to change."

Quark President, Tim Gill

# Changing the World

In 1982, computer scientists John Warnock and Charles Geschke were employees at Xerox Corporation in Palo Alto, California. Xerox was a leader in **faxing**, copying, printing computers, and office supplies. At the time, printing at home was tedious and difficult. **Dot matrix** printers were bulky, noisy and very basic. Sometimes they printed off the page; other times, text might run randomly adrift. Special **typesetting machines**

**OPPOSITE:** Dot matrix printers commonly created errors when printing type.

could produce higher-quality copies but cost $10,000 or more per unit.

Geschke and Warnock worked in the research and development department—the Palo Alto Research Center (PARC). They wrote computer programs for Xerox's Star, which was meant to be an all-in-one workstation with embedded word processing and graphics capabiltiy.

The two developed a computer program called Interpress. It could read and track the exact locations of any object on a digital page, meaning that a printed document looked exactly as it did on the computer screen. Xerox needed computers, but didn't fully understand them since they weren't popular. Apple's first desktop computer, the Macintosh, was still two years away. Xerox wasn't convinced that Interpress would be helpful. "We spent months traveling around to all the divisions within Xerox and back to corporate selling this idea," Warnock said. Finally, Xerox agreed to use Interpress but wouldn't announce its invention until every Xerox product had it. That would take years. Its creators knew computers and Interpress were the future. They couldn't wait.

Charles Geschke

Warnock and Geschke, along with other PARC employees, left Xerox. In December 1982, Adobe was founded. The company was named after Adobe Creek, a stream near Warnock's home, where their first office was located. Early on, Steve Jobs, the founder of Apple, visited. He was familiar with their work at PARC and offered to buy the start-up, but they turned him down. Two years later, Adobe released PostScript, an evolved version of Interpress.

eatures like different **fonts**, sizes or columns couldn't be computer generated in the early days. Publishers had to print out pictures and blocks of text separately, then cut them out and paste them on a larger board. Steve Jobs adopted PostScript early on. It was slow and tedious. PostScript gave creators control over the layout of their documents. It used mathematics to scale, rotate, and move objects around the page. Before this, every letter in a font was the same width—a "t" was as wide as a "w." PostScript allowed letters and numbers to have varying widths, giving them character and artistry. They called their font library Type 1. Computer and printer manufacturers quickly jumped at the chance to add the program to their products, and soon people at home could make their own newsletters, signs, and other professional-looking printouts.

Apple founder, Steve Jobs

**OPPOSITE** The stylized "A" in Adobe's logo was designed by Marva Warnock.

Jobs was an early adopter of PostScript. He included it in his LaserWriter machine, a nearly $7,000 printer with a powerful built-in computer. In just a few years, PostScript became the international standard for desktop publishing.

Warnock's wife, Marva, was a graphic designer. He noticed that she spent a lot of time making manual changes. Type had to be printed out and pasted into place, and graphics had to be hand-drawn. Any changes or mistakes meant the designer had to start over from scratch. PostScript used a design language to create curves, sizes, and other features on a page. Designers would use this language to tell PostScript what they wanted, but the process was tedious. There were no dedicated applications. Designers had to input equations and code manually, hoping they got it right.

In 1985, work on Adobe Illustrator began, and it was released in 1987. Designers could finally draw circles, curves, and anything else they imagined—

and see these changes in real time. They controlled every detail on the page without writing code.

Photoshop became Adobe's next big hit. Thomas and John Knoll began working on it in 1987. Thomas as an engineer and amateur photographer who wrote a program that converted the bright green monochrome images on his father's Apple II Plus computer to grayscale. John, who was working at George Lucas' Industrial Light

## Out of Toner

Before copy machines, people used carbon paper or mimeograph machines, which pressed wet ink through a stencil onto paper. Xeroxing kept ink off people's fingers, allowing them to copy documents cleanly by using a dry, granular ink and a powder called toner, made of plastics, dyes, and other additives that produced a glossy or **matte** finish. First developed in 1942, the first Xerox photocopier debuted in 1959. In 1960, a commercial aired showing that making copies was so easy, even a chimpanzee could do it!

An Apple LaserWriter machine

John Knoll of ILM

and Magic. The Knoll brothers collaborated to create a program called Image Pro—later named PhotoShop and then simply Photoshop. Knoll pitched the idea to roughly 30 companies before Adobe bought it in 1988. Photoshop enabled users to retouch photos, clone sections of an image to overlay on other areas, and use other special effects tools to refine images.

In 1990, Warnock launched the Camelot Project. He wanted to shift from paper to digital documents. However, computers at the time used different applications and operating systems. Fax machines allowed people to send files and print them out, but they were usually low quality. Warnock believed there should be a way to share high-quality documents that could be read on any computer and printed on any printer. In 1993, Adobe Acrobat 1.0 debuted. Its Portable Document Format—or

## The Font Wars

Apple's first Macintosh had only a few fonts preloaded fonts. They were low-resolution and quickly became **pixelated** when enlarged. Apple saw what Adobe was doing, however. They didn't want Adobe's fonts to be the only options. Instead, Apple created its own font library, called TrueType, which allowed people to scale fonts up and down in size. Microsoft later purchased TrueType and installed it on their Windows computers. While regular users favored TrueType for its familiarity, professionals in the print and design industries preferred the flexibility of Type 1 fonts. Eventually, both companies released their specifications, allowing everyday users to create their own fonts at home. In 1997, OpenType was released as a joint project between Microsoft and Adobe, effectively ending the "font war."

PDF—was a universal file format that allowed users to view, print, edit, and share documents with anyone who had a computer.

PDFs didn't catch on immediately, even after Adobe Acrobat Reader was made available for free. Adobe's board of directors even considered scrapping the program, but Warnock fought back. He knew that businesses would understand PDF's value once they learned how paper costs would decrease. And eventually, they did. By 2020, there were more than 2.5 trillion PDFs in the world.

**OPPOSITE** The goal for PDFS was to create a universal file format that preserved fonts, images, and layouts across all devices and platforms.

Adobe had already secured a foothold in the desktop publishing market by absorbing competitor Aldus in 1994, forming Adobe Systems Inc. Aldus's program, PageMaker, was widely used by home users, but publishing professionals preferred QuarkXPress. In 1998, Quark's CEO offered to buy Adobe. It wasn't a serious offer. Quark was a small, privately owned company that didn't have the $1.6 billion to buy Adobe. Instead, the move was a message: Quark was prepared to compete for the number-one spot.

Rather than intimidate Adobe, the offer pushed them to work even harder. "Our response was, we're going to be d***ed if we get taken over by these turkeys," Warnock said. "We're going to annihilate them. We'll just out-engineer them." Adobe also had something that Quark didn't: Apple's support.

PDF

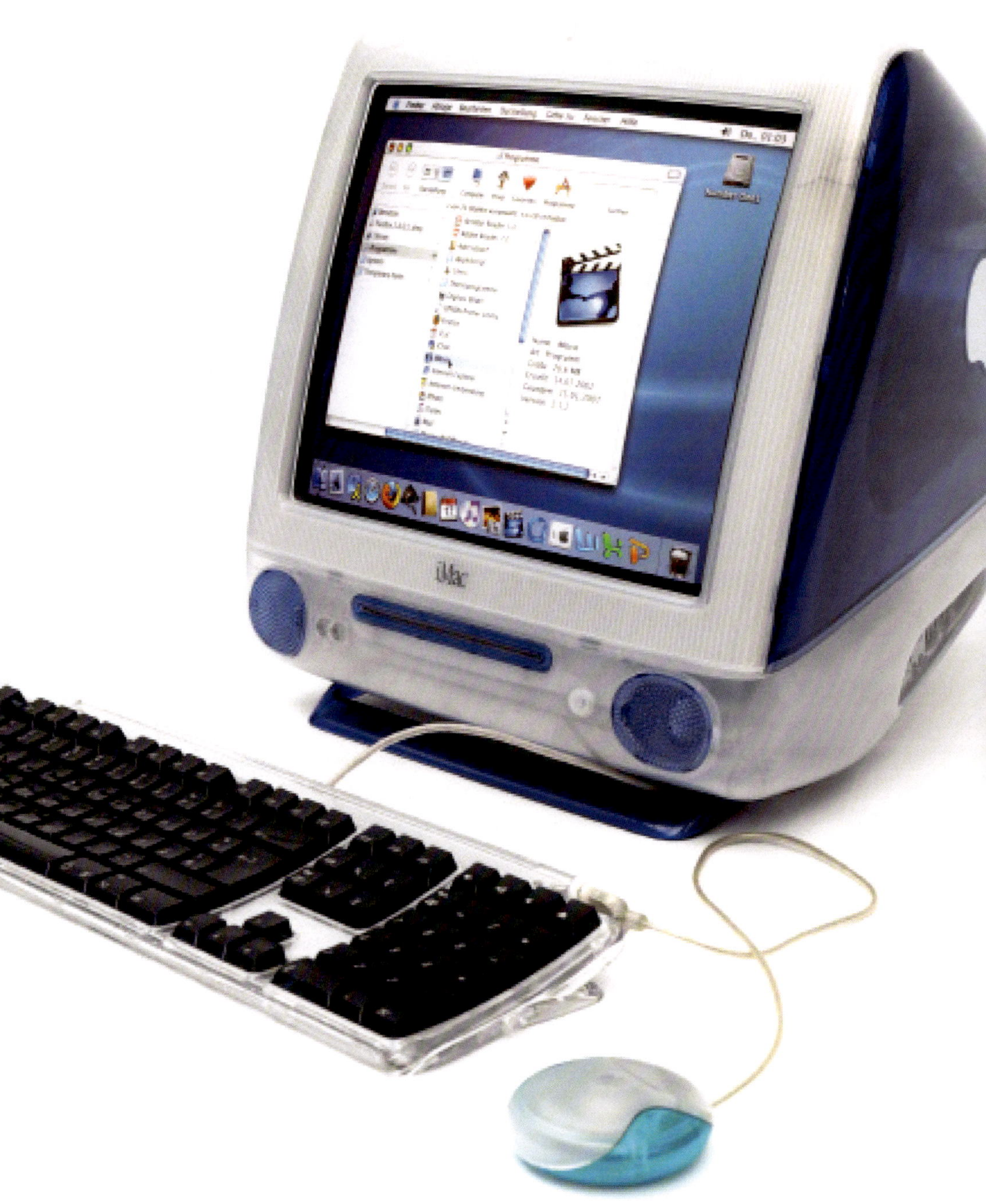


Early support from Apple was influential in Adobe's success

InDesign ran on Apple's new OS X system, released in 2002, while Quark stuck with the Mac Classic operating system, betting that users wouldn't want to upgrade. When QuarkXPress 5 was released later that year, its lack of new features disappointed many. The following year, Adobe Creative Suite launched with Photoshop, Illustrator, and InDesign. Its cost was just a little more than half the cost of Quark Express. Quark lost its grip on publishing as XPress faded and Adobe surged ahead.

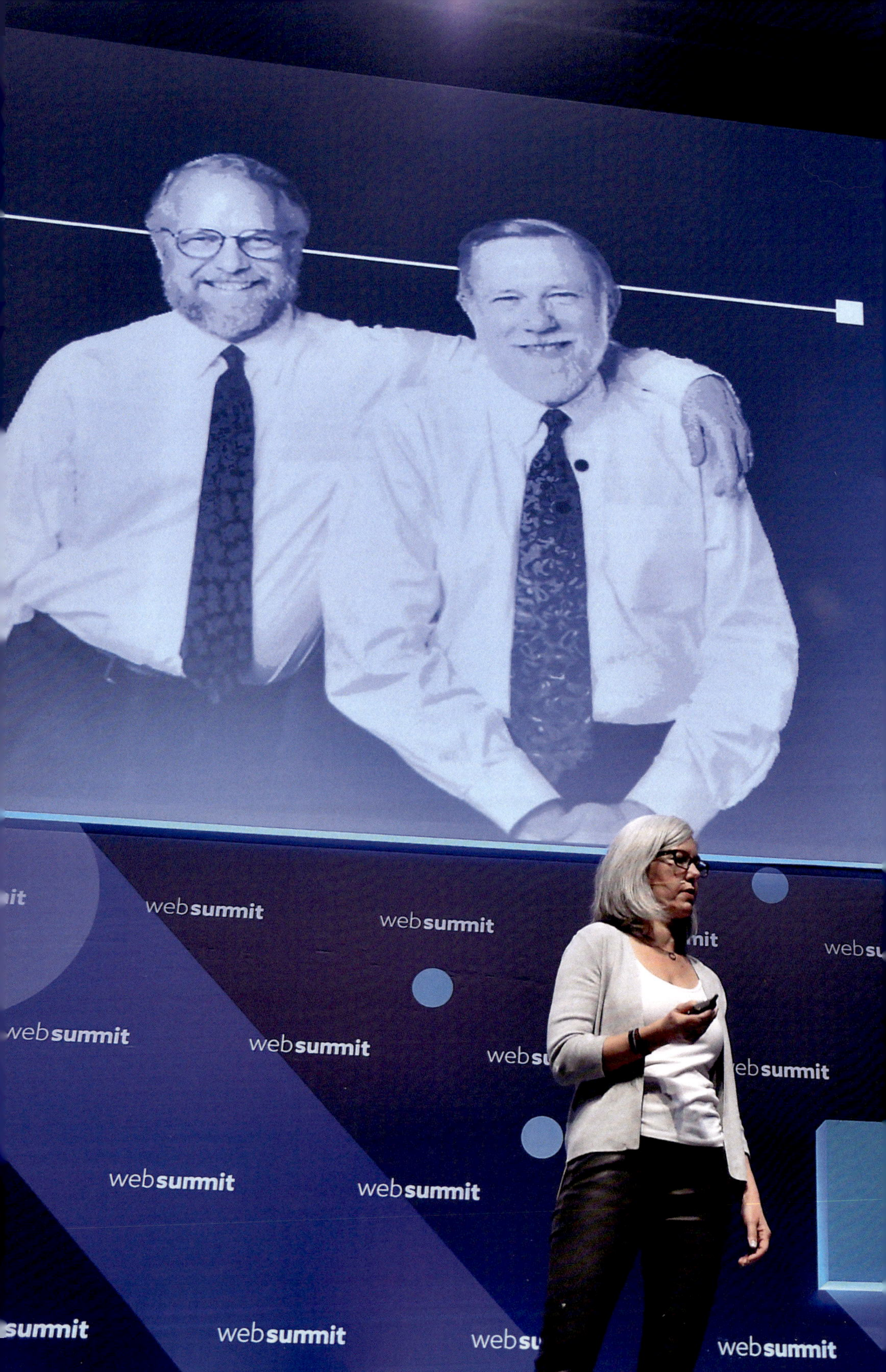
websummit
websummit
websummit
websummit
websummit
websummit
websummit
websummit

## Save As

In 2023, Adobe's value was estimated at $235 billion. It is one of the largest and most diverse information technology companies in the world. But that success would not have come without leaders and workers who believed in the products they made.

John Warnock was Adobe's first president during its first two years. He then became Chief Executive

**OPPOSITE:** Adobe's tools are so widespread that more than 90% of creative professionals globally use them in some form.

Officer, filling that role for another 16 years. He retired in 2001, although he continued as a member of the company's board of directors until 2017. He continued inventing and held 20 patents at the time of his death in 2023. "Being a CEO of a company that is over $1 billion is not all it cracked up to be," he said. "The thing I really enjoy is the invention process. I enjoy figuring out how to do things other people don't know how to do." In 1997, Warnock's son, Chris, commissioned a font in honor of his father. Adobe type designer Robert Slimbach created Warnock Pro. It's an old-fashioned-looking font that is both authoritative and inviting.

Charles "Chuck" Geschke was the CEO from 1986 to 1994. He later served as Adobe's president from 1989 to 2000. He and Warnock co-ran the company with humility and a shared desire to create new things. Their goal was to build a company they genuinely believed in, where everyone clearly understood its purpose. Geschke strove to keep meetings to a minimum while juggling the interests of all stakeholders and community spaces. They also wanted to train more leaders ready to step up when needed.

In 2006, Geschke and Warnock were awarded the AeA Annual Medal of Achievement Award from the American Electronics Institution, an honor given based on the legacy they have made in the technology industry. They were the first software executives ever to receive that honor. In 2008, they were presented with the National Medal of Technology and Innovation, the nation's highest honor for technological achievements. They received the award at the White House, presented by President Barack Obama.

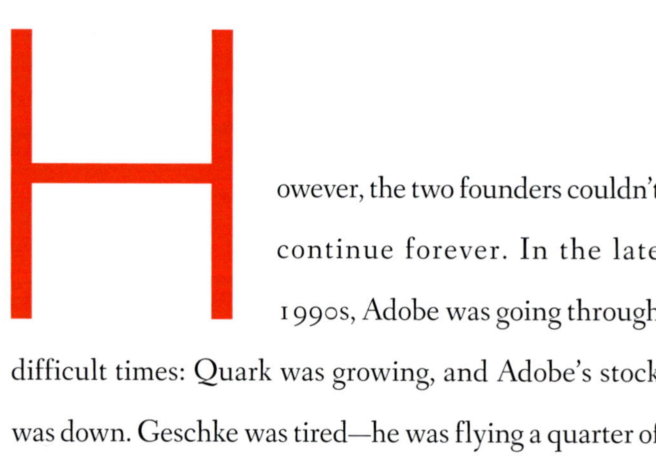

However, the two founders couldn't continue forever. In the late 1990s, Adobe was going through difficult times: Quark was growing, and Adobe's stock was down. Geschke was tired—he was flying a quarter of a million miles every year for meetings. He and Warnock hired several possible successors and eventually settled on Bruce Chizen. Chizen had joined the Adobe family in 1994 as a division head, quickly rising through the ranks until he took over as CEO in 2000. Some people were skeptical. Chizen wasn't a doctor, an engineer, or

## For Ransom

The Geschke family lived a low-key, modest lifestyle; however, thanks to media attention, Adobe's value was widely known. In 1992, Geschke suffered a harrowing ordeal. On May 26, he left for work as usual and, as he pulled into the Adobe parking lot, he was kidnapped at gunpoint by two men. They held him for five days, threatening his family and neighbors. Geschke managed to escape once, but he was quickly recaptured. The kidnappers then instructed Geschke's daughter, Kathy, to deliver $650,000 in ransom money. The drop was arranged, and the FBI tracked the kidnappers back to their hideout. Geschke was eventually rescued, physically unharmed, though the ordeal left a lasting impact on him.

a traditional businessman, but Geschke and Warnock chose him because he was willing to embrace new ideas.

At that point, Adobe was a $1.2 billion company. Chizen vowed to grow the company to even greater heights. Digital cameras and camera phones capable of taking both photos and videos were becoming popular among professionals and everyday users. Photoshop Elements was released to give average users the basic Photoshop tools—such as image resizing and

Bruce Chizen

editing—at one-sixth the price of regular Photoshop, prompting many to eventually upgrade.

Creative Suite was also launched during Chizen's tenure. It offered new features, such as working with higher-resolution images, a more streamlined image-location tool, and the **Counterfeit** Deterrence System, which prevented people from illegally minting money.

In 2005, the company acquired Macromedia, Inc., a graphics company credited with creating programs like Flash and Dreamweaver. These programs made building websites easier. Flash let users embed and play videos on websites. YouTube, created around the same time, used Flash. Macromedia had also recently signed deals with cell phone companies Nokia and NTT DoCoMo to create interactive content, while Adobe had already been working with NTT DoCoMo to integrate PDF readers into phones.

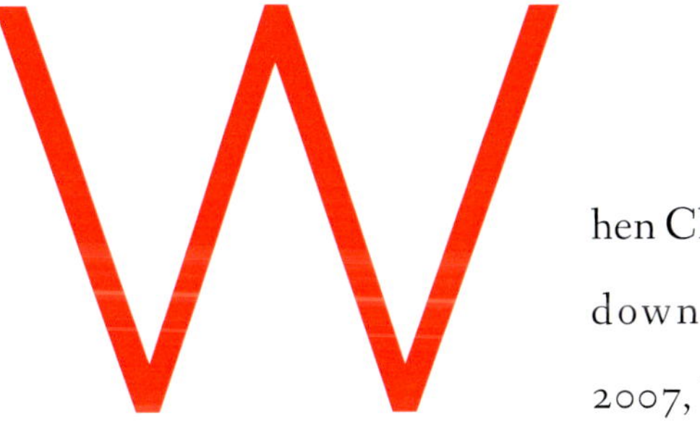

hen Chizen stepped down as CEO in 2007, Warnock and Geschke were ready. They chose Shantanu Narayen as the next successor. His work enabled the Adobe transition from desktop software to **cloud** services. Adobe Creative Cloud was released in 2012 and the subscription subscription service allows users to access Creative Suite components through the cloud rather than paying a large one-time licensing fee. Users can also choose individual Adobe products and pay a monthly fee. Narayen has also guided Adobe through acquisitions involving e-commerce software, marketing software, and a web analytics company. Between 2008 and 2021, Adobe's revenue grew from $3.58 billion to $15.79 billion.

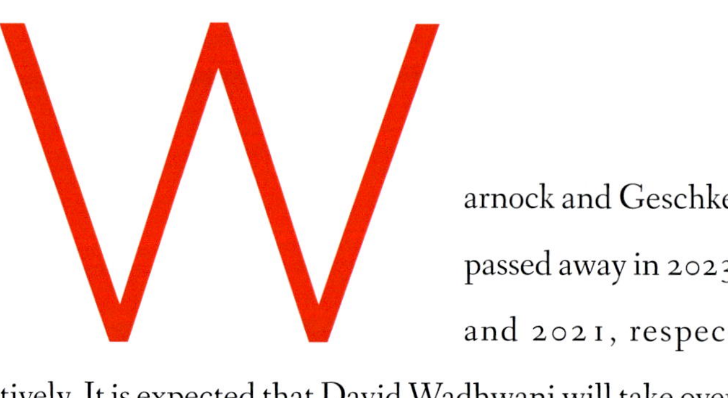

Warnock and Geschke passed away in 2023 and 2021, respectively. It is expected that David Wadhwani will take over as CEO after Narayen. In 2022, Wadhwani played a role

## Fortune 500

Adobe became a Fortune 500 company in 2017, sliding in at spot 443. The list, compiled by Fortune magazine, ranks the 500 largest corporations in the United States by revenue. Collectively, these companies account for about two-thirds of the country's **gross domestic product** and nearly $19 trillion in revenue. More than 31 million people worldwide are employed by Fortune 500 companies. In 2024, the top five Fortune 500 companies were Walmart, Amazon, Apple, UnitedHealth Group, and Berkshire Hathaway, a conglomerate managed by CEO Warren Buffett. That same year, Adobe ranked 233.

in Adobe's acquisition of Figma, a collaborative interface design app and Adobe's largest investment to date.

Executives aren't the only voices at Adobe. The company's Adobe for All programs equip employees with skills and confidence to advance at work and home. Adobe Digital Academy helps people switch careers by providing the education and experience needed for new roles. Their India-specific SheSparks internship program helps women return to full-time work after a career break. **Mentorship**, support groups, training, and opportunities help women regain their footing in the corporate world.

The Adobe For All Summit

Adobe Leadership Circles and the Women's Executive Shadow Program also target women's advancement, and the Adobe Leader Experience provides flexible training sessions.

The Adobe For All Summit conference lets employees attend either in person or online. Sessions, labs, and training help users develop proficiency in Adobe products, while digital leaders, engineers, product managers, and software architects connect with other professionals in the field.

# Innovations

Adobe has maintained a culture of inclusion and excellence since Geschke and Warnock's early days. The company occupies spots on lists such as LinkedIn's Best Workplaces for Innovators, Forbes' List of the World's Best Employers, and Fortune 100's Best Companies to Work For. It offers employee resource groups, programs that support new ideas, and professional development opportunities. Adobe also encourages employees to find solutions for social and environmental challenges, with prizes awarded to the winners.

In 2023, Adobe employees raised more than $33 million through personal donations paired with Adobe's grant and matching programs. More than 9,500 organizations worldwide benefited, and employees contributed over 200,000 hours of volunteer time.

Going digital cuts paper waste and a company's carbon footprint. For every 1 million pages signed digitally using Adobe Acrobat Sign, more than 27 million gallons (102.2 million liters) of water and 1.5 million pounds (0.7 million kilograms) of waste are avoided. In 2023, Adobe customers opened over 400 billion PDFs and signed more than 8 billion documents.

Adobe Founders Tower

Adobe has also set ambitious sustainability goals. It spearheaded a plan to power 100 percent of its operations with renewable energy and to achieve **net zero** by 2050. Its 18-story Founders Tower, located at its San Jose, California headquarters, is energy-efficient and fully electric.

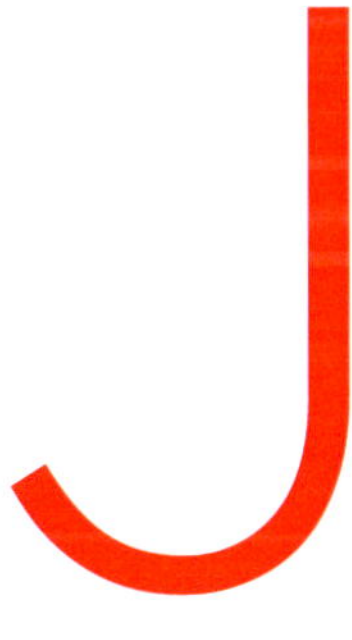

UST Capital frequently ranks Adobe as a top company for paying sustainable wages, offering parental leave, committing to environmental initiatives, and focusing on charity—all while maintaining high profits.

In 2018, Adobe achieved global pay parity, ensuring that employees in the same job and location were paid equally regardless of gender, race, or ethnicity. Globally, women represented more than 35 percent of employees in 2023 and 57 percent of new hires. More than 27 percent of leadership roles are filled by women, and these numbers have grown year over year.

## Data Farms

Moving from paper-based services to cloud-based services sounds like a great green idea—but that data still has to be stored somewhere. Data centers are physical facilities that house data on high-performance computers. They are energy hogs, using 10 to 50 times more energy than an office building of similar size, and they produce a great deal of heat, warming the surrounding environment. Data-heavy technologies, such as AI, will only add to the burden, with global electricity usage projected to jump from 1 percent to 9 percent. Northern Virginia hosts the largest concentration of data centers in the world, housing servers for Google, Amazon, and Microsoft.

InDesign
F
A
Arial
Narrow Bold
*R-4899_Catalog
7
8

Adobe leads in diversity and inclusion, earning Forbes' Best Employer for Diversity, ranking in the Diversity Best Practices Inclusion Index, and scoring 100 from the Human Rights Campaign.

owever, Adobe has also faced its fair share of controversies. Its Solution Partner Program comprises partners who train people and companies to best utilize Adobe's digital experience. Between 2011 and 2020, Adobe allegedly paid partners tied to the United States government a percentage of the software's purchase price. This was viewed as **kickbacks** since those partners influenced whether government departments would purchase other Adobe products. In 2023, Adobe paid $3 million to resolve the issue.

In early June 2024, Adobe users received a pop-up notice alerting them to an update to Adobe's General Terms of Use. The notice stated that Adobe could "access your content through both automated and manual methods, such as for content review." Many interpreted this as Adobe strong-arming its way into private and personal information. Users worried about what Adobe would do with their photos, documents, and files or whether their work might be used to train AI or if Adobe was spying on them. Adobe insisted it would not use users' content for spying or to train AI. It clarified that it would not take over users' work. Nevertheless, both the Adobe community and Adobe employees voiced their concerns.

Later that same month, the **Federal Trade Commission** filed a complaint against Adobe, Maninder Sawhney, and David Wadhwani. The complaint alleged that Adobe pushed customers toward an annual paid monthly subscription rather than a yearly model. At first glance, the preselected monthly option may seem

## Buying Power

According to Unilever, one-third of consumers are more likely to buy from brands that they believe are doing social or environmental good. Nearly 90 percent of people are more likely to buy from companies that support issues they care about, while 76 percent refuse to buy from companies with opposing views. After the terms of service and subscription controversies, Adobe's stock dropped by as much as 18 percent, indicating that investors were unimpressed with the company's handling of the situation. However, Adobe's revenue increased by 11 percent by the end of the year, bolstered by its new AI tools and cloud services.

attractive to customers seeking a lower upfront cost or those still deciding whether a yearlong subscription is worth it. However, a hidden early termination fee—50 percent of the remaining monthly payments through the year—meant anyone canceling within 12 months had to pay it. The cancellation process was also problematic, with dropped calls and chats causing some customers to think they had canceled, only to find Adobe still charging them.

Ado
dobe
xpress
he quick and easy
e-anything app. Free.

## Toward the Future

Adobe celebrated its 40th anniversary in 2022—a huge milestone since few tech companies last this long. More than 80 percent of the companies featured in a 1993 edition of the Soft-letter 100—a once-prominent ranking system—have since gone out of business or been acquired by larger companies. Adobe was ranked number seven on that list.

**OPPOSITE:** Adobe is integrating AI and machine learning into its products to help automate tasks like image tagging, content-aware editing, and even generating design suggestions.

In 2023, Adobe celebrated 30 years of PDFs. In February of that year, Adobe merged with Microsoft, bringing PDF capabilities to 1.4 billion Windows users. (Note: While Adobe and Microsoft have indeed formed strong partnerships to integrate Acrobat PDF technology into Microsoft Edge, there has been no actual merger.) Acrobat was the top PDF viewer on Google Chrome, helping billions of people open files.

arch 2023 was a big month. At Adobe Summit 2023, the company made several major

# I Photoshopped It

As Photoshop became more popular, it entered mainstream language as a descriptive verb. It was far easier to say "I Photoshopped it" than "I digitally altered this image." "Photoshop" was added to the Merriam-Webster dictionary in 2008. Photoshop has become part of everyday language, spawning Photoshop competitions, photoshopped celebrity photos, and even references in song lyrics and movie plots. Adobe itself has not endorsed the use of "photoshop" as a verb; when brands become part of common language, trademark rights can be diluted or even lost. Examples include linoleum, taser, and xerox.

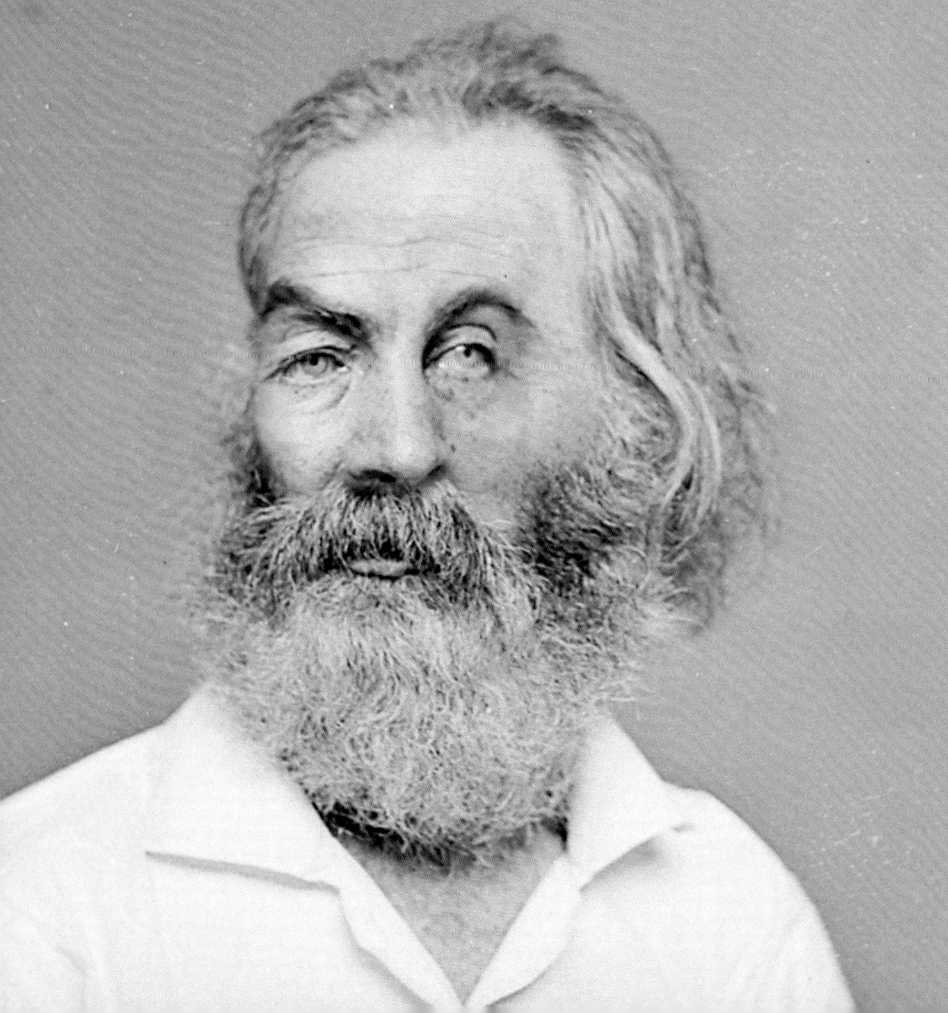

AI generated Bob Ross and robot

announcements. Its next path forward was generative AI—Firefly, the first in a family of creative generative AI models. Generative AI is a form of artificial intelligence that can create new content (ChatGPT is one example). Adobe had already stepped into AI with Adobe Sensei, an AI and machine learning (ML) technology that could mine data, streamline workflows, and detect patterns in customer behavior. Firefly was designed to work alongside Sensei: Firefly would enhance creative output while Sensei provided context for the information Firefly retrieved.

Generative AI can help businesses customize advertisements for each potential buyer. It can ease the strain on creative teams that must devise multiple approaches to advertise a product by generating various content

**OPPOSITE** Photoshop AI generated image from the first verse of the song "America the Beautiful."

versions. It can also produce new content faster than a person could.

However, there are downsides. Generative AI remains a new and unrpoven tehcnology is a new and unproven technology. Adobe promises big results, but if people are too hesitant to use it, those results might never materialize in the data. Adobe initially gave its generative AI product away free, aiming to build a customer base before charging a fee.

AI is still largely uncharted territory and some people are reluctant to try it. Some fear it will eventually replace human workers, as it already reuses pre-existing creative material to generate new content. Artists have been outspoken about what they see as outright theft. Others worry that AI could produce deepfake videos, track browsing without consent, or cause harm through faulty decisions. Only time will tell whether Firefly, Sensei, and other generative AI products will succeed or fail.

In December 2023, Adobe attempted to acquire the start-up design company Figma for $20 billion. Figma was founded to bring easy website and app design to a wide audience. Adobe once tried to branch out and compete with Figma through its product, XD, but XD never gained the same popularity. Adobe tried to buy Figma in 2020 and 2021 but ultimately backed down.

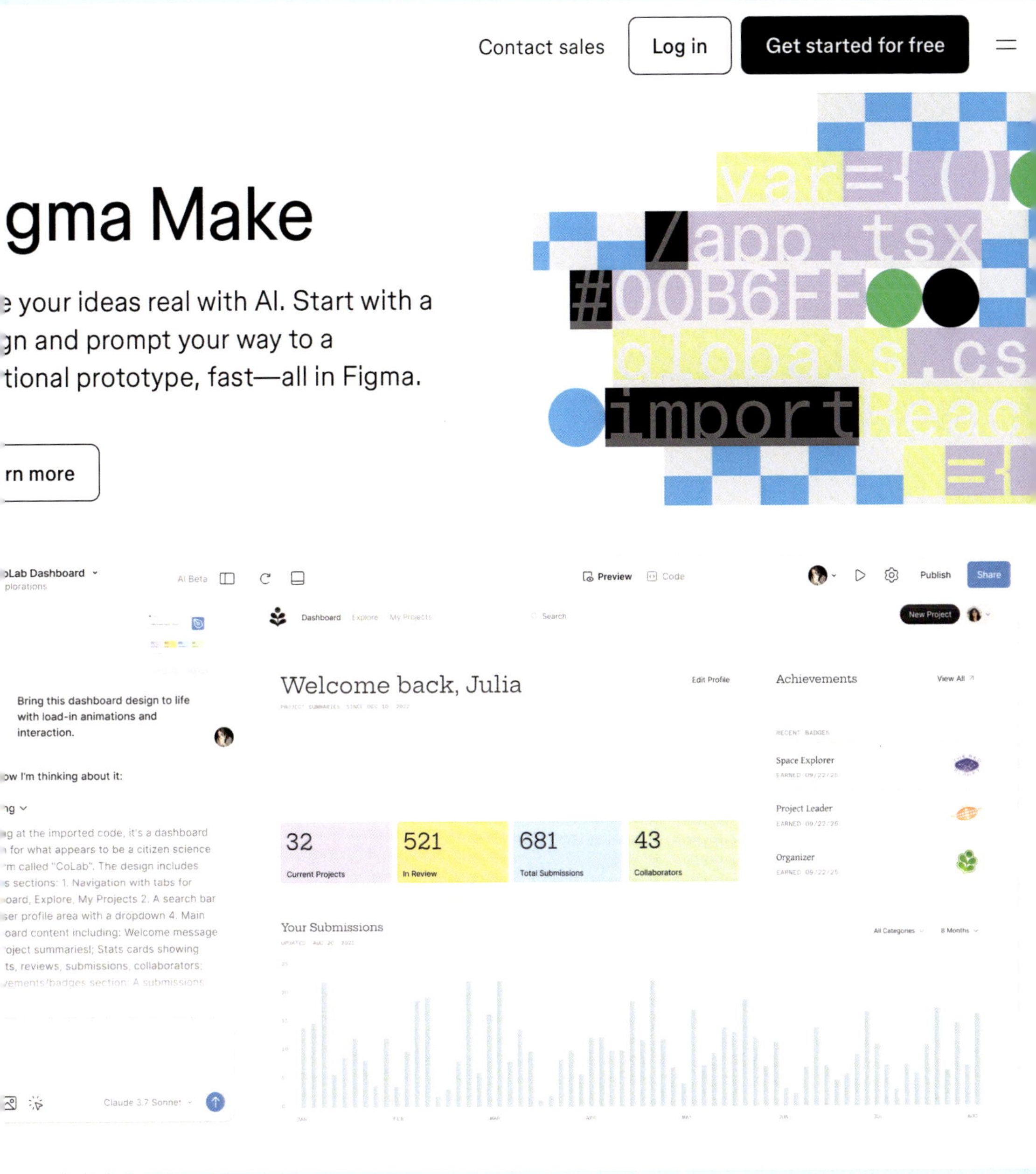

Contact sales
Log in
Get started for free

# gma Make

e your ideas real with AI. Start with a
gn and prompt your way to a
tional prototype, fast—all in Figma.

rn more

var={()
/app.tsx
#00B6FF
globals.cs
import Reac

oLab Dashboard
plorations

AI Beta

Preview
Code
Publish
Share

Dashboard
Explore
My Projects
Search
New Project

Bring this dashboard design to life with load-in animations and interaction.

ow I'm thinking about it:

ng

ng at the imported code, it's a dashboard
 for what appears to be a citizen science
m called "CoLab". The design includes
s sections: 1. Navigation with tabs for
oard, Explore, My Projects 2. A search bar
ser profile area with a dropdown 4. Main
oard content including: Welcome message
oject summaries]; Stats cards showing
ts, reviews, submissions, collaborators;
vements/badges section; A submissions

Claude 3.7 Sonnet

Welcome back, Julia

Edit Profile

| 32 | 521 | 681 | 43 |
|---|---|---|---|
| Current Projects | In Review | Total Submissions | Collaborators |

Achievements
View All

RECENT BADGES

Space Explorer
EARNED 09/22/25

Project Leader
EARNED 09/22/25

Organizer
EARNED 09/22/25

Your Submissions

All Categories
8 Months

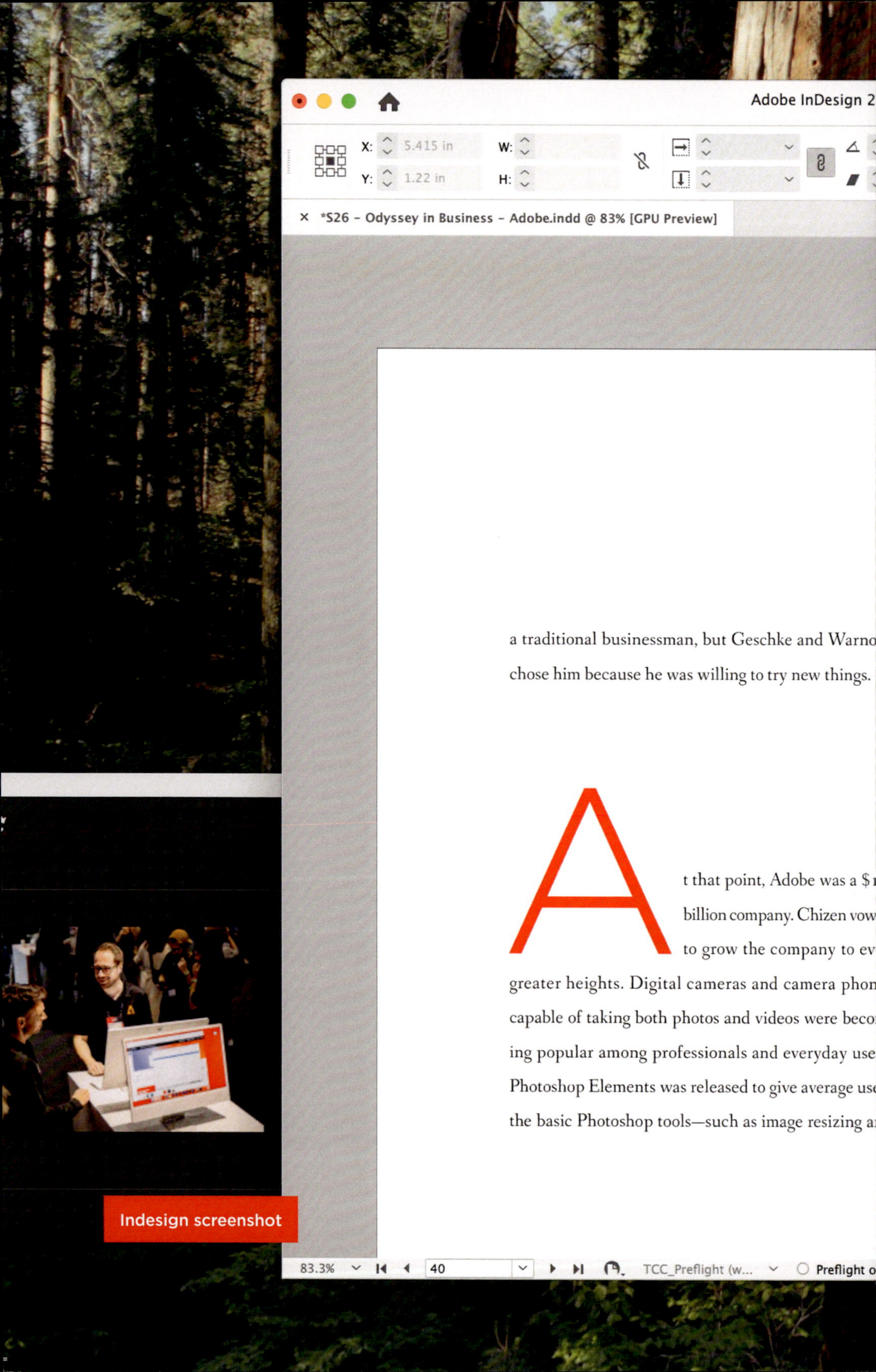

Indesign screenshot

Adobe InDesign 2

X: 5.415 in
Y: 1.22 in
W:
H:

*S26 – Odyssey in Business – Adobe.indd @ 83% [GPU Preview]

a traditional businessman, but Geschke and Warno
chose him because he was willing to try new things.

At that point, Adobe was a $1
billion company. Chizen vow
to grow the company to ev
greater heights. Digital cameras and camera phon
capable of taking both photos and videos were beco
ing popular among professionals and everyday use
Photoshop Elements was released to give average use
the basic Photoshop tools—such as image resizing a

83.3% 40 TCC_Preflight (w... Preflight o

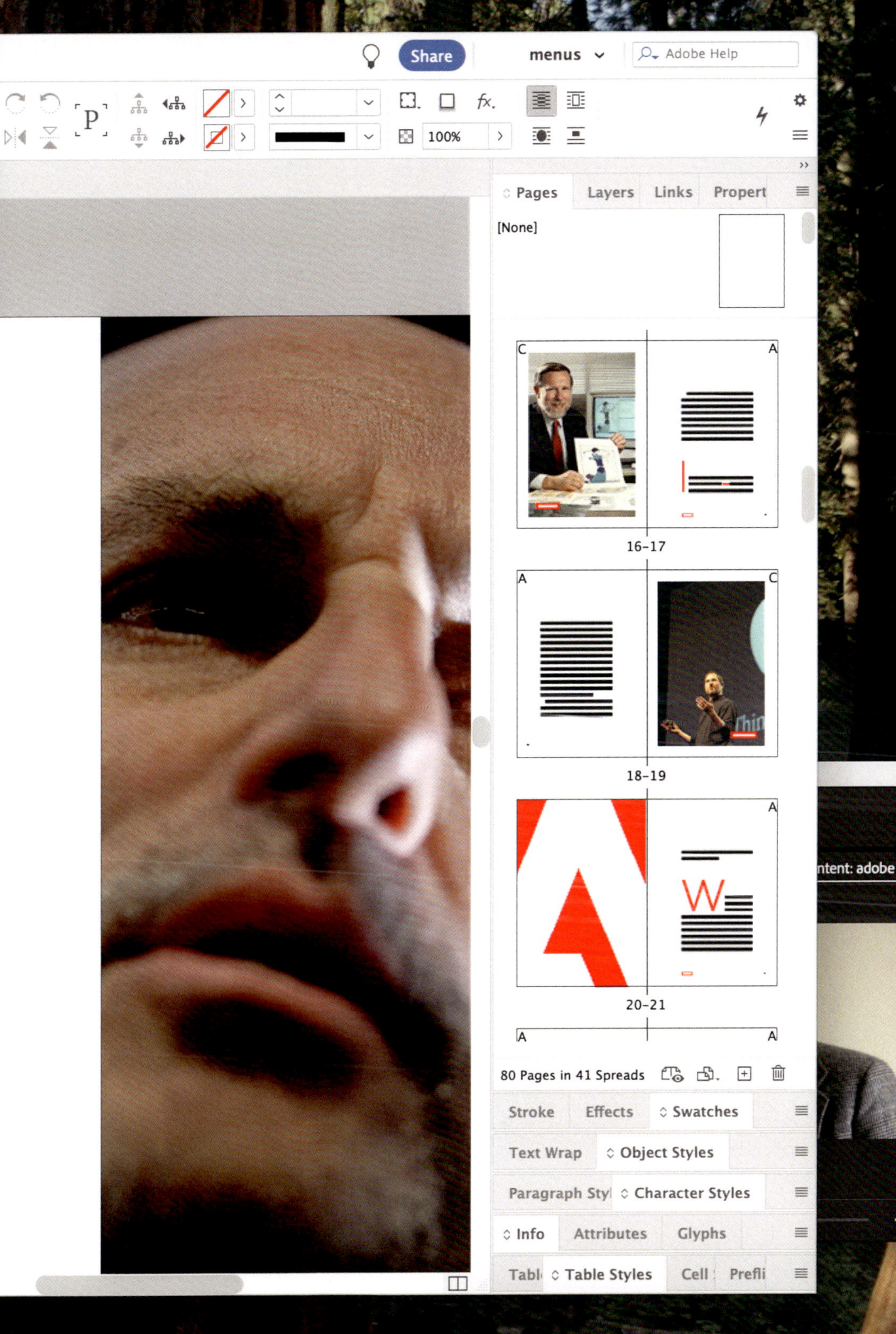

Share
menus
Adobe Help
100%
Pages
Layers
Links
Propert
[None]
C
A
16–17
A
C
18–19
A
20–21
A
A
80 Pages in 41 Spreads
Stroke
Effects
Swatches
Text Wrap
Object Styles
Paragraph Styl
Character Styles
Info
Attributes
Glyphs
Tabl
Table Styles
Cell
Prefli
ntent: adobe

The week before announcing the merger, Adobe quietly canceled "Project Spice," a product that would have competed with Figma.

owever, regulators in Europe had been closely monitoring acquisitions. Britain's Competition and Markets Authority argued that the two companies could be direct rivals, and that the takeover would eliminate competition and give Adobe a **monopoly**. Shareholders were disappointed becausee the buyout buyout would have given them a huge windfallMany Figma users were relieved, having chosen Figma because of its differences from Adobe's offerings. Ultimately, the two companies mutually agreed to call off the deal, and Adobe was forced to pay a $1 billion termination fee.

Adobe lost its chance in website and app development but continued supporting creatives in other fields. Adobe Premiere Pro has become essential in the music and film industries. Stars like Lil Nas X, Childish Gambino, Madonna, Ariana Grande, and Beyoncé have used it to create music videos. Disney even called it a "pivotal moment in video editing" in its *Light & Magic* documentary about the history of motion picture and visual effects.

As of 2025, Adobe Creative Cloud offers more than 20 creative apps used by filmmakers, photographers, designers, animators, website builders, business professionals, and more. From simple PDFs to complex AI assistants, Adobe will continue pushing the envelope to expand the digital world. "Regardless of changes in technology, the mission of the company has remained the same—change the world through digital experiences," CEO Shantanu Narayen said. "It comes down to recognizing what our customers need and not being afraid to change because—at the end of the day—preserving the status quo is not a business strategy."

## Photoshop Ethics

The ethics of retouching photos is complex. With filters, retouching apps, and even Photoshop readily available, the temptation to tweak images is undeniable. Pictures of flawless celebrities, gorgeous landscapes, and even AI-generated images abound. But where is the line between removing a pimple and promoting unhealthy beauty standards? Some celebrities, such as Zendaya, Lady Gaga, and Jameela Jamil, have spoken out against excessive photoshopping. Some countries, such as France, have enacted Photoshop laws that require a disclaimer stating that a photo has been retouched. Violations can lead to up to six months in prison and a 75,000-Euro fine.

# Selected Bibliography


About Adobe. Accessed December 19, 2024. https://www.adobe.com/about-adobe.html

Apple Inc. "Seybold 1998 San Francisco." Internet Archive. September 1, 1998. https://archive.org/details/vhs-steve-jobs-1998-seybold-seminars-480p

Berlin, Leslie. *Troublemakers: Silicon Valley's Coming of Age*. New York: Simon & Schuster, 2017.

Lamkin, Bryan. "Evolution of the Digital Document: Celebrating Adobe Acrobat's 25th Anniversary." Adobe Blog. June 14, 2018. https://blog.adobe.com/en/publish/2018/06/14/evolution-digital-document-celebrating-adobe-acrobats-25th-anniversary

Laskevitch, Stephen. *Adobe Photoshop: A Complete Course and Compendium of Features*. San Rafael, CA: Rocky Nook Inc., 2020.

Walsh, Joyce. *Graphic Design Essentials*. New York: Bloomsbury Publishing, 2020.

# Glossary

**Analyst** A professional who examines data or systems to provide insights, evaluations, or solutions

**Application** A software program designed to perform specific tasks on a computer or device

**Carbon footprint** The total amount of greenhouse gases produced directly or indirectly by an individual, organization, or product

**CEO** The Chief Executive Officer, who is the highest-ranking person in a company and responsible for overall strategy and decision-making

**Cloud** A network of remote servers used to store, manage, and process data over the internet

**Counterfeit** A fake copy of something valuable or official, made to deceive or defraud

**Desktop publishing** The creation of documents using page layout software on a personal computer for print or digital formats

**Dot matrix** A type of computer printer that forms characters using rows of tiny dots

**Faxing** Sending documents electronically over a telephone line using a facsimile machine

**Federal Trade Commission**
A U.S. government agency that protects consumers and ensures fair business practices

**Font**
A specific style and size of typeface used in written or printed text

**Graphic design**
The art and practice of combining images, text, and ideas to communicate visually

**Gross domestic product**
The total value of goods and services produced within a country in a given time period

**Kickback**
An illegal payment made in return for favorable treatment, often in business or government

**Licensing fee**
A payment made to legally use someone else's intellectual property or product

**Matte**
A non-glossy finish that reduces light reflection on surfaces like paper, photos, or paint

**Mentor**
An experienced person who offers guidance, support, and advice to someone less experienced

**Monopoly**
The exclusive control of a market or service by a single company or entity

**Net zero**
A state in which greenhouse gas emissions are balanced by removals, resulting in no net increase

**Pixelate**
To blur or obscure an image by displaying it in enlarged, visible pixels

**Typesetting machine**
A device that arranges text for printing by automatically assembling characters in a specific layout

# Websites

### Adobe Facts for Kids

https://www.astrosafe.co/article/adobe
Learn more about Adobe and what it does.

### Adobe Fast Facts

https://www.adobe.com/about-adobe/fast-facts.html
A quick overview of Adobe and its history.

### PostScript: A Digital Printing Press

https://computerhistory.org/blog/postscript-a-digital-printing-press/
Explore the story of PostScript from the Computer History Museum.

# Index

acquisitions ,44, 72
Adobe initiatives
  Adobe For All, 45, 46, 47
  Adobe Digital Academy, 45
  Adobe Leadership Circles, 47
  SheSparks, 45
  Solution Partner Program, 55
  Women's Executive Shadow Program, 47
Adobe products
  Acrobat, 27, 29, 49, 62
  Creative Cloud, 43, 73
  Creative Suite, 33, 42, 43
  Firefly, 65, 68
  Illustrator, 22, 33
  InDesign. 10, 30, 33, 70
  PDFs. 29, 43, 49, 62, 74
  Photoshop. 23, 27, 33, 40, 42, 63, 67, 75
  Photoshop Elements. 40
  PostScript. 17, 18, 21, 22
  Premiere Pro .73
  Project Spice, 72
  Sensei, 65, 68
Adobe Summit, 62
Aldus, 30
Apple computers and software
  Apple II Plus, 23
  LaserWriter, 21, 24
  Mac Classic, 33
  Macintosh, 15, 28
  OSX, 33
artificial intelligence (AI)
  generative AI, 65, 67, 68
awards, 37, 38
Camelot Project, 27
Chizen, Bruce, 39, 40, 41, 43
data centers, 53
ethics, 75
Figma, 45, 68, 69, 72, 73
font libraries
  TrueType, 28
  Type 1, 18, 28
Fortune 500, 45
Founders Tower, 50, 51
Geschke, Charles, 13, 16, 17, 36, 37, 38, 39, 40, 43, 44, 48
Geschke, Kathy, 39
Interpress, *See* PostScript
Jobs, Steve, 10, 17, 18, 19, 21
Knoll, John and Thomas, 23, 26, 27
Macromedia, Inc.
  Dreamweaver, 42
  Flash, 42
Narayen, Shantanu, 43, 44, 74
Nokia, 42
NTT DoCoMo, 42, 43
Obama, Barack, 38
OpenType, 28
printers, 13, 18, 21, 27
Quark, 9, 10, 11, 30, 33, 38
Seybold Conference, 9, 10,
Slimbach, Robert, 36
Wadhwani, David, 44, 57
Warnock, Chris, 36
Warnock, John, 9, 13, 14, 15, 17, 27, 29, 30, 35, 36, 37, 39, 40, 43
Warnock, Marva, 21
Windows, 28, 62
Xerox, 13, 14, 15, 17, 23, 63
YouTube, 42